The Artist's Way
Morning Pages Journal

The Artist's Way Morning Pages Journal

A Companion Volume to
The Artist's Way

Julia Cameron

Jeremy P. Tarcher/Putnam
a member of
Penguin Putnam Inc.
New York

Jeremy P. Tarcher/Putnam
a member of
Penguin Putnam Inc.
375 Hudson Street
New York, NY 10014
www.penguinputnam.com

First Trade Paperback Edition 1997
Copyright © 1995 by Julia Cameron

Library of Congress Cataloging-in-Publication Data
Cameron, Julia.
    The artist's way morning pages journal: a companion volume to
The Artist's Way/Julia Cameron.
        p. cm.
    Jeremy P. Tarcher/Putnam
    ISBN 0-87477-886-7 (acid-free paper)
    1. Artist's block. 2. Artists—Psychology. 3. Creation
(Literary, artistic, etc.)   I. Title.
    N71.C27 1995   95-23431 CIP
701'.15—dc20

Photograph of Julia Cameron © 1996 by Aloma; photograph of
Mark Bryan by Mike McDermott
Cover design by Lee Fukui
Cover illustration, *Cranes Flying by Mount Fuji* (mid-1790s),
by Nagasawa Rosetsu (1754–1799). Private collection.
Printed in the United States of America

20 19 18 17 16 15 14 13

Contents

Introduction to

The

Artist's Way

Journal

*I*n the little room where I write, I have two views. The first is of the Sangre de Cristo Mountains. The second is of something nearly as tall: the wooden bookcase where I keep row after row of journals, the same size and shape as the one you are holding in your hands.

Those rows of journals contain morning pages for the last twelve years or so. They contain my thoughts and my second thoughts: my friendship with Laura, my fight with an obstinate academic faculty, my decision to live in London for a while, my worries about my father's health, and finally, the details of my father's death. In short, those journals have listened to me. They have been company on my life's travels. I am indebted to them for clarity, consolation, advice, and humor. They have kept me sane.

The journal you hold in your hands is first and foremost intended as just such a companion. Through it, you will be contacting yourself: your hopes, fears, dreams, aspirations, and the simple daily flow of life. Through it, you will find privacy, a sort of portable "room of your own" where your opinion is off the record, except to your own eyes.

Although you may have kept a journal previously, you are asked to keep this one in a very specific way: through the daily use of morning pages. Note the words *daily* and *morning.*

What, exactly, are morning pages, and why should you use them?

Put simply, morning pages are three pages of longhand morning writing. They are to be written strictly off the top of your head. (No "real" writing, please!) Pages may sound whiny, grumpy, even petty. Occasionally, a brilliant idea may sparkle through, but more often it will be "Need to do the laundry, forgot to call my sister, wonder how Dad is."

When I am in a puckish mood, I call morning pages "Brain Drain." They are used to siphon off whatever nebulous worries, jitters, and pre-occupations stand between me and my day. I am reminded of a won-derful old television commercial that portrayed test driving "on the

Baja Peninsula." As the truck bucked and lurched over rugged terrain, the windshield wipers went "thunk, thunk, thunk," clearing away the dirt and debris that obscured the windshield. *That* is what morning pages are: spiritual windshield wipers.

Once we get those muddy, maddening, confusing thoughts on the page, we face our day with clearer eyes. We are more honest with ourselves and others, more centered, and more spiritually at ease. For this reason, I often say that morning pages are a form of meditation. You are writing down the "cloud" thoughts that drift across your mind. In writing them down, you clear them.

Unlike more focused journal writing, you do not set a topic for morning pages. Typically, many topics will appear. They may tumble all over one another, arriving on the page in a disorganized heap of fragmentary thoughts. That's fine. Please don't judge them or yourself.

The writing of morning pages is just early-morning thinking set down on the page. Very often, that thinking will feel jumbled up. Remember: these are our wake-up thoughts, nothing more. Again, do not try to "write" here!

A day at a time, a page at a time, we wipe clear our vision of the world. We see what obstacles impede us, what roads are open to us. We become more alert to the shortcuts, switchbacks, and dangers of the trail. In short, we become present to our lives, at once more alive in guiding them and more receptive to signposts that indicate alternate routes. We become explorers rather than mere tourists.

"Making a word trail," I call it. The trail leads inward to the self and outward to the world. By retracing it, we can double-check our thinking. By continuing it, we can expand that thinking and allow it to guide us further still.

"Morning pages are like getting up in the morning and telephoning yourself," one practitioner puts it.

I would take that a step further. Not only are you contacting yourself, you are also contacting your *Self*. Over a period of time, the pages lead to a deepening sense of inner wisdom and a sustaining belief in the benevolence of universal flow.

What do I mean by that?

Morning pages prioritize the day. They create a sort of slipstream that allows us to move through life with greater ease, conscious of a more fortuitous intermeshing of our inner and outer worlds. I do not know precisely *why* this is so, but I do know *that* it is so. Still, I would not ask you to trust me on this. I would rather ask you to experiment.

Write three pages a day. Write them first thing in the morning, whether you are "really" awake or not. Yes, do write your pages by hand. Many of us have experimented with "cheating" on a computer, and the resultant pages simply are not the same. Speaking for myself, computer pages have seemed to generate speed and distance, but not as much depth. With each day's pages we map our consciousness. Like early maps, our cartography is done by hand. Writing by hand yields us a handmade life. That is our goal.

To certain practitioners, morning pages may at first seem alarmingly negative. "All I do is gripe!" you may exclaim, not wanting to create negativity or perpetuate it by looking it in the face. Jungians may have an easier time of it with this shadow dancing. Remember that you are not so much "encountering the shadow" as just buying it a cup of coffee and letting it put its two cents in early instead of darkening your entire day.

Morning pages are powerful. You may experience them as a river. You may also experience them as a boat. Through the morning pages, you will encounter the propulsion of creative flow underlying and informing all life. That flow may feel so strong that you will need the morning pages to travel comfortably in its celerity.

Morning pages are intended both to provoke and comfort. In them, we ask questions, but we also receive our answers. The "still, small voice" is amplified when we go inside to hear it.

Clarity is a fruit of morning pages. We know what's bothering us and why. Over time, we learn what we'd like to do about it. The pages even afford us rehearsal space until we choose to act. Remember that we all recover at our own pace.

A word about "recovery" is in order here. It is my belief that the ideal is to re-cover the distance we have drifted from our authentic creative selves. Morning pages are a powerful way to do that. However, in order to work at maximum effectiveness, morning pages are best used in conjunction with a second tool, the artist date. And so, even though this is a morning pages journal, let me explain the matching tool.

Put simply, the artist date is a one- to two-hour block of time set aside weekly for an excursion on your own that celebrates and nurtures your creative self. These excursions, or play dates, should be festive. Don't do what you "should" do. Do what sounds like fun. You are learning a habit of planning risk and expansion on your artist's behalf.

First you see a French film on an artist date.

Then you take a class on the French Impressionists.

Then you go to France.

You may also find that on artist dates you experience a sense of well-being. It is as though you have built a radio kit. With morning pages, you are sending. With artist dates, you feel the thrill of being contacted back.

Viewed in this way, my morning page journal is a history of my spiritual connection. By moving my hand across the page, I move the hand of the universe across my life.

Introduction

to

Contract

*A*s a mark of commitment to yourself and your process, we ask you to sign a contract acknowledging your intent to undertake a creative recovery.

Contract

I, _____, commit myself to the daily process of morning pages. Additionally, I commit to a weekly artist date. I understand that these two tools are most powerful when used in conjunction, and I commit myself to using both together.

I, _____, further understand that working with these tools may create deep change, some of it turbulent. I commit myself to excellent self-care—adequate sleep, diet, exercise, and self-valuing. Above all, I commit to honoring the validity for me of my own unique perceptions—for the duration of the twelve weeks ahead and hopefully long after.

_____
(signature)

_____
(date)

Creativity flourishes in an atmosphere of safety and acceptance. That is the atmosphere you will be building for yourself through the morning pages. The sense of this safety may not be immediate. In fact, undertaking morning pages may feel both exciting and scary. Will I really find the time? What if I have nothing to say? You *will* have "something" to say—even if that something is merely griping at committing to the pages.

It is the artist date that many of you may find more tricky. It sounds so frivolous. What good could that do?

Exactly this. Artist dates reinforce your sense of safety. They strengthen your contact with a source of benevolence in the world at large. When you write morning pages you are like a person in a life raft sending out a signal: "Here. Here I am. This is what I want." But until you take your artist date, it is as if you have your receive channel shut off. In other words, you may SOS, but when the call comes back, "Tell us again, *exactly,*" you don't hear it. You leave yourself marooned and feeling frightened. *Please* practice both tools together.

We speak of practicing the morning pages and practicing the artist date. You do not need to use either tool perfectly. Be gentle but persistent in your attempts. Here are the answers to some often-asked questions:

Yes, morning pages should be done in the morning. Yes, it's better to do pages "late" than not at all. (And yes, everyone is tempted to cheat a little.)

As for the artist dates, they are easily sabotaged. A friend may ask to come along. A deadline may suddenly rear its head. Be vigilant about protecting your artist date. Plan it ahead of time, execute it, and consider it a major victory no matter how frivolous it may seem at the time.

Your sense of safety will grow, along with your sense of mastery over these basic tools.

*1. There is no wrong way
to do morning pages. These
daily morning meanderings
are not meant to be art. (p.10)*

2. Morning pages map our own interior. Without them our dreams may remain terra incognita. (p. 15)

3. The morning pages move us into artist brain. Artist brain is our inventor, our child, our very own personal absent-minded professor. Artist brain says, "Hey! That is so neat!" It puts odd things together.... (p. 13)

4. The morning pages miniaturize our Censor. The Censor is part of our leftover survival brain. Any original thought can look pretty dangerous to our Censor. (p. 13)

5. Morning pages will allow you to detach from your negative Censor. It may even begin to seem like a grumpy cartoon character. (p. 13)

6. Doing your artist date, you are receiving—opening yourself to insight, inspiration, guidance. (p. 13)

7. When we work at our art, we dip into the well of our experience and scoop out images. Because we do this, we need to learn how to put images back. How do we fill the well? By the artist date. (p. 21)

_____

_____

_____

_____

_____

_____

_____

_____

_____

_____

_____

_____

_____

_____

_____

_____

_____

_____

_____

_____

_____

_____

_____

_____

_____

_____

_____

_____

_____

_____

_____

_____

_____

8. Unfortunately, many artists never receive critical early encouragement. As a result, they may not know they are artists at all. (p. 25)

9. Too intimidated to become artists themselves, very often too low in self-worth to even recognize that they have an artistic dream, many people become shadow artists instead. Artists themselves but ignorant of their true identity, shadow artists are to be found shadowing declared artists. (p. 27)

10. Artists love other artists. Shadow artists are gravitating to their rightful tribe but cannot yet claim their birthright. (p. 27)

11. In recovering from our creative blocks, it is necessary to go gently and slowly. What we are after here is the healing of old wounds—not the creation of new ones. (p. 29)

12. Judging your early artistic efforts is artist abuse. (p. 29)

13. Most of the time when we are blocked in an area of our life, it is because we feel safer that way. (p. 30)

Negative beliefs are exactly that: beliefs, not facts. Artists need not be drunk, crazy, broke, alone—or any of a number of our culture's negative beliefs about them. (p. 31)

14. *It is possible, quite possible, to be both an artist and romantically fulfilled. It is quite possible to be an artist and financially successful. (p. 33)*

15. Affirmations help achieve a sense of safety and hope: I am a channel for God's creativity, and my work comes to good. (p. 36)

16. My dreams come from God and God has the power to accomplish them. (p. 36)

17. My creativity heals myself and others. (p. 36)

_____
_____
_____
_____
_____
_____
_____
_____
_____
_____
_____
_____
_____
_____
_____
_____
_____
_____
_____
_____
_____
_____
_____
_____
_____
_____
_____
_____
_____
_____

18. There is a divine plan of goodness for my work. (p. 37)

19. I am willing to let God create through me. (p. 37)

20. It is important to remember that at first flush,
going sane feels exactly like going crazy. (p. 41)

21. As we gain strength, so will some of the attacks of self-doubt. This is normal, and we can deal with these stronger attacks when we see them as symptoms of recovery. (p. 41)

*O*ne of the first fruits of morning pages is a clearer sense of personal identity. You are starting to look with clearer eyes at how you see yourself and how you see the world around you. You may feel a sense of wonder as your true self is slowly revealed. Skepticism may be starting to give way to curiosity. Who exactly are you? As your identity gets clearer, you will find your relationships shifting. You may be starting to know and speak your mind, which makes you less easy to take advantage of, more capable of saying no. Your more poisonous playmates will not appreciate this shift in your self-worth.

Many creative people surround themselves with "crazymakers," those who discount their realities, abuse their schedules, expect special treatment, break their agreements, and generally, create chaos, which siphons off creative energy. As you recover your identity these crazymakers may feel threatened. "You're getting selfish," they may tell you.

In the very best sense, they are right. Your self is beginning to be more visible, less embedded in the expectations of others. This can be threatening, not only to others but to you as well. Treat yourself carefully. Remember that "treating yourself like a precious object will make you strong."

It may take strength to execute your pages this week—strength in the face of your crazymakers, strength in the face of your own possible temptation to return to the person who was blocked. "Better safe than sorry," part of you may say.

I remind you: you were both safe *and* sorry. That is the identity you are in the process of shedding. Now that you are no longer who you were but not yet who you are becoming, you may find yourself feeling awkward, like a hatchling. Hatchlings *are* awkward, but they are also becoming free.

22. Remember, the morning pages are private and are not intended for the scrutiny of well-meaning friends. (p. 42)

23. *Creativity flourishes when we have a sense of safety and self-acceptance.* (p. 42)

24. Not surprisingly, the most poisonous playmates for us as recovering creatives are people whose creativity is still blocked. (p. 42) Do not expect your blocked friends to applaud your recovery. (p. 43)

25. Be very careful to safeguard your newly recovering artist. A related thing creatives do to avoid being creative is to involve themselves with crazymakers. (p. 43) Crazymakers are those personalities that create storm centers. (p. 44)

26. The crazymakers in your life share certain destructive patterns that make them poisonous for any sustained creative work. Crazymakers break deals and destroy schedules. Crazymakers expect special treatment. Crazymakers discount your reality. Crazymakers pretend you're crazy. (p. 47)

27. Crazymakers spend your time and money. Crazymakers are expert blamers. Crazymakers create dramas—but seldom where they belong. (pp. 47, 48)

28. *Crazymakers hate schedules—except their own. (p. 48)*

29. As frightening and abusive as life with a crazymaker is, we find it far less threatening than the challenge of a creative life of our own. (p. 49)

30. Perhaps the greatest barrier for any of us as we look for an expanded life is our own deeply held skepticism. (p. 49)

31. The reason we think it's weird to imagine an unseen helping hand is that we still doubt that it's okay for us to be creative. (p. 50)

32. When our little experiment provokes the universe to open a door or two, we start shying away. (p. 51)

33. We've gotten brave enough to try recovery but we don't want the universe to really pay attention. (p. 51)

*34. Think of the mind
as a room. In that room
we keep all of our usual
ideas about life. (p. 51)*

35. The room has a door. That door is ever so slightly ajar, and outside we can see a great deal of dazzling light. (p. 51)

36. Nudging the door open a bit more is what makes for open-mindedness. (p. 51)

37. We can gently set aside our skepticism—for later use, if we need it—and when a weird idea or coincidence whizzes by, gently nudge the door a little further open. (p. 51)

38. Attention is an act of connection. (p. 53)

39. The truth is that a creative life involves great swathes of attention. Attention is a way to connect and survive.
(p. 52)

40. The reward for attention is always healing. (p. 53)

*41. Remember that it is far harder
and more painful to be a blocked
artist than it is to do the work.*
(p. 55)

42. Be alert, always, for the presence of the Great Creator leading and helping your artist. (p. 55)

Whⁿen Mark and I teach a twelve-week course, we often refer to week three by shorthand. "It's Anger Week," we say. One of the first ways that our creative power returns to us is as anger.

"But I'm *not* angry," some students snap back, sparks flying from between their teeth.

Maybe it isn't anger. Maybe it's something closer to self-respect. As the morning pages build up, clearing your vision of the present, you also get a sharper look at your past. This can make for both clarity and volatility.

As you work to put your daily life in order, bits and pieces of your past may surface, including memories of times and people to whom you gave away too much of yourself.

"I wasted so much time!" you may catch yourself thinking. And then, "Other people *really* wasted my time!"

When this wave of clarity happens, you may see that you have been powerful enough to have survived a great deal of negativity, but that you aren't interested in taking that negativity anymore. Often to your own surprise, you may find yourself speaking up:

"No, it's not okay you're late."

"No, I have a real issue with lending you money."

"No, I'm not sick, crazy, selfish. I'm just *fed up* with being your battery!"

Oops! Some of this does sound like anger, even though it is more accurately a simple reclaiming of misplaced power. Many of you may feel this power in your bodies as a sort of heightened voltage. Therefore:

This is a week to focus on concrete self-nurturing acts: food in the refrigerator, cleaning out those bathroom shelves, tossing the clothes that signal low self-worth, or better yet, passing hand-me-down castoffs into the arms of Goodwill.

Practice being specific with yourself. Admit what you'd like to change. Claim your artist date and some extra "mulling" time. Remember, experience is also a form of treasure. As you experience your present and reexperience your past, you are sorting the dross from the gold and naming yourself worthy. That self-valuing is the source of your power.

43. Anger points the way, not just the finger. In the recovery of a blocked artist, anger is a sign of health. (p. 61)

44. We're much more afraid that there might be a God than we are that there might not be. (p. 63)

45. *If there is a responsive creative force that does hear us and act on our behalf, then we may really be able to do some things. (p. 64)*

46. *Never ask whether you can do something. Say, instead, that you* are *doing it. Then fasten your seat belt. (p. 65)*

47. The universe falls in with worthy plans and most especially with festive and expansive ones.
(p. 65)

48. We like to pretend it is hard to follow our heart's dreams. The truth is, it is difficult to avoid walking through the many doors that will open. (p. 66)

49. The universe is prodigal in its support. We are miserly in what we accept. (p. 66)

50. Leap, and the net will appear. (p. 66)

51. Making a piece of art may feel a lot like telling a family secret. (p. 67)

52. *The act of making art exposes a society to itself.* (p. 67)

53. Often we are wrongly shamed as creatives. From this shaming we learn that we are wrong to create.
(p. 69)

54. Criticism that asks a question like "How could you?" can make an artist feel like a shamed child. (p. 69)

55. Not all criticism is shaming. In fact, even the most severe criticism when it fairly hits the mark is apt to be greeted by an internal Ah-hah! if it shows the artist a new and valid path for work. (p. 69)

56. It often takes another artist to see the embryonic work that is trying to sprout. The inexperienced or harsh critical eye, instead of nurturing the shoot of art into being, may shoot it down instead. (p. 70)

57. We cannot make our professional critics more healthy or more loving or more constructive than they are. But we can learn to comfort our artist child over unfair criticism; we can learn to find friends with whom we can safely vent our pain. We can learn not to deny and stuff our feelings when we have been artistically savaged. (p. 70)

58. Art requires a safe hatchery. (p. 70)

59. We must learn that when our art reveals a secret of the human soul, those watching it may try to shame us for making it. (p. 70)

60. It is God's will for us to be creative. (p. 71)

61. Pointed criticism, if accurate, often gives the artist an inner sense of relief. The criticism that damages is that which disparages, dismisses, ridicules, or condemns. (p. 72)

62. Useless criticism
leaves us with a feeling
of being bludgeoned.
There is nothing to
be gleaned from
irresponsible criticism.
(p. 72)

63. Many blocked people are actually very powerful and creative personalities who have been made to feel guilty about their own strengths and gifts. (p. 73)

*B*y this point in your work with the morning pages, you may have experienced some substantial inner shifts. For many, these shifts manifest as moving the furniture—mentally *and* physically. I call this shift "spiritual chiropractic."

Your sense of space or your sense of color may have altered. Your musical tastes may have taken a new turn. You might be experiencing vivid dreams and daydreaming about new possibilities in a more expansive way. Some of you may now sense you have outgrown a job, an apartment, even a romance. In short, you are deepening into a new sense of integrity.

In order to facilitate this deepening, you may wish to do a week of media deprivation. By limiting the inflow of other people's words and ideas, it is possible to focus more clearly on your own. Without reading, talk radio, or television, you are able to hear yourself think. What that self has to say is often very interesting.

Your goals may be clearer, your likes and dislikes more sharply drawn. For some of you this may be a little frightening, as if life without its familiar blurred edges can look awfully dramatic.

Relax. You do not need to force sudden changes. Instead, try thinking of your pages as a boat. Know that you are being carried forward; know that your destination will suit you. Above all, allow yourself to speculate on the light, not merely the dark. What classes sound fun? What skills and hobbies sound as though you'd enjoy them? Let your imagination play with these ideas. The new you and the old you may differ on diversions.

Especially if you undertake media deprivation, you may wish to use your week to undertake small, self-nurturing projects: mending the socks, organizing the kitchen shelves; cleaning under the kitchen sink; going through the closets; giving your niece the wrong-for-me-but-right-for-her cache of makeup you've been hoarding.

Remember that it is you, as told to you by *you,* that we are listening for now. That is the meaning of integrity.

64. *Growth is an erratic forward movement: two steps forward, one step back. (p. 74)*

65. Be alert for support and encouragement from unexpected quarters. (p. 75)

66. Experiment with solitude. (p. 75)

67. Extreme emotions of any kind—the very thing that morning pages are superb for processing—are the usual triggers for avoiding the pages themselves. (p. 80)

68. We are tempted, always, to reverse cause and effect: "I was too crabby to write them," instead of, "I didn't write them so I am crabby." (p. 80)

69. The morning pages perform spiritual chiropractic.
They realign our values. (p. 80)

70. In order to have self-expression, we must first have a self to express. (p. 80)

71. The process of identifying a self invariably involves loss as well as gain. (p. 81)

72. In addition to posing problems, the pages may also pose solutions.

(p. 81)

73. Faced with impending change, change we have set in motion through our own hand, we want to mutiny. (p. 81)

74. Creativity is grounded in reality, in the particular, the focused, the well observed, or specifically imagined. (p. 82)

75. We become original because we become something specific: an origin from which work flows. (p. 82)

76. You are your own promised land, your own new frontier. (p. 83)

77. By tossing out the old and unworkable, we make way for the new and suitable.

(p. 83)

78. Just as travelers on a jet are seldom aware of their speed unless they hit a patch of turbulence, so, too, travelers on the Artist's Way are seldom aware of the speed of their growth. (p. 84)

79. Each day's morning pages take a swipe at the blur you have kept between you and your real self. (p. 84)

80. Conditioned as we are to accept other people's definitions of us, this emerging individuality can seem to us like self-will run riot. (p. 84)

81. You may well be experiencing a sense of both bafflement and faith. You are no longer stuck, but you cannot tell where you are going. (p. 84)

82. *What you will learn to do is rest in motion, like lying down in a boat. Your morning pages are your boat. They will both lead you forward and give you a place to recuperate from your forward motion.*
(p. 85)

83. The morning pages symbolize our willingness to speak to and hear God.
(p. 85)

84. *"I trust my perceptions" is another powerful affirmation to use as we undergo shifts in identity. "A stronger and clearer me is emerging." (p. 86)*

By this week, you may find yourself playing an emotional game of eenie-meenie-miney-moe as you toy with new possibilities. You may alternate between giddy elation over your newly rediscovered freedom and a stubborn itch to dig your heels in and change nothing. Such vacillating is normal. You are learning to balance the energies of expansion and change with your own needs for safety and the familiar.

Another way to put this is to remind you of Alice, who ate the magic mushroom that changed her size. Some days you will feel very big. Others, you will feel quite small. In other words, you are learning to balance what is possible now with what may be possible in the long run.

Such shape-shifting is an integral part of the process you are engaged in. Your sense of possibility may become very elastic as you realize that your previously accepted limits were far more arbitrary than you had imagined. Which size do you really want to be?

Realizing your own dizzying potential may create a sense of velocity. Just hang on. Rapids are followed by calmer waters, and you too will soon find a more cohesive, if expanded, sense of self.

This newer, larger self may require more time and space than your previous self. Conversely, it might shift from an isolationist into someone capable of greater intimacy. The possibilities are diverse.

For example, if your pattern has been to oversacrifice your own life for the comfort of others, you may find such self-sabotaging behaviors increasingly hard for you to indulge. Congratulations! You are escaping the virtue trap.

As you shed false niceties, you will find yourself capable of forging more authentic relationships. Your expanded self expects the possibility of genuine reciprocity. In love, in friendship, in work, and in play, your expanded self may rightfully expect the possibility of joy.

85. As recovering creatives, we often have to excavate our own pasts for the shards of buried dreams and delights. (p. 86)

86. If you feel stuck in your life or in your art, few jump starts are more effective than a week of reading deprivation.
(p. 87)

87. No reading? That's right: no reading. (p. 87)

88. Reading deprivation casts us into our inner silence. (p. 87)

89. Don't read. If you can't think of anything else to do, cha-cha. (p. 89)

90. One of the chief barriers to accepting God's generosity is our limited notion of what we are in fact able to accomplish. (p. 91)

91. We define as grandiose many schemes that, with God's help, may fall well within our grasp. (p. 91)

92. Remembering that God is our source, we are in the spiritual position of having an unlimited bank account. (p. 91)

93. Since everyone can draw on the universal supply, we deprive no one with our abundance. (p. 92)

94. Remembering that God is our source, an energy flow that likes to extend itself, we become more able to tap our creative power effectively. (p. 92)

95. *We must learn to let the flow manifest itself where it will—not where we* will *it. (p. 92)*

96. The desire to be worldly, sophisticated, and smart often blocks our flow. Spirituality seems too naive. (p. 93)

97. Creativity is a spiritual issue. Any progress is made by leaps of faith, some small and some large. (p. 93)

98. What dream are you discounting as impossible given your resources? What payoff are you getting for remaining stuck at this point in your expansion? (p. 94)

99. Experiment with this two-step process: ask for answers in the evening; listen for answers in the morning. Be open to all help. (p. 94)

100. *The shift to spiritual dependency is a gradual one. (p. 94)*

101. Dependence on the creator within is really freedom from all other dependencies. Paradoxically, it is also the only route to real intimacy with other human beings. (p. 95)

102. Recovery is the process of finding the river and saying yes to its flow, rapids and all. (p. 95)

103. As you come to trust and love your internal guide, you lose your fear of intimacy because you no longer confuse your intimate others with the higher power you are coming to know. (p. 96)

104. While the "footwork" is necessary, it seldom pays off in a linear fashion. It seems to work more like we shake the apple tree and the universe delivers oranges. (p. 96)

105. An artist must have downtime, time to do nothing. (p. 96)

*I*n order to believe in abundance, we must believe in an abundant God; if not a personal, anthropomorphic God, then an abundant universal flow, one which can come to us from any direction, not merely from our designated source of choice.

Practicing this week's morning pages can become a meditation on the abundance already existing in your life. The pages can be a place to note the luxuries that could cheer you—a pint of raspberries, real marmalade, an hour of classical music. Resolve to make a place for them this week.

So often, we mistake abundance with our monetary bottom line. Many times our sense of deprivation comes from lack of sleep, lack of time, lack of intimacy with our loved ones, all commodities we can control the flow of.

Abundance is not rooted in our checkbooks. It is rooted in our system of checks and balances: the care we expend on ourselves versus the care we expend on others; the light heart we gain from pursuing our dreams versus the darkened heart that comes from keeping company with our fears.

We find ourselves at this point with one foot in each world. One foot belongs to our believer, fully capable of walking on water or on fire. The other foot, the one we play hopscotch with, belongs to our nonbeliever, and that foot is scared we are on thin ice.

Money is a reality. If, for one week, you will count and record your spending, clarity will begin to accumulate on the many ways you may sell yourself short. No cash for fresh flowers? Maybe your flower money went for that diner burger where you felt oppressed by the noise as well as the greasy food.

The point of counting is to realize the abundance on life's menu. At its simplest, a menu is a selection of choices. All of life may be seen the same way. By focusing on our power to choose—our ideas, our companions, our pastimes, and our passsions—life becomes a menu for abundance and we become our own master chefs.

What if you packed a mini-picnic to the office? A half hour in the closed office with fresh flowers, fresh raspberries, and a meditation tape can make not only the lunch but life seem a little bit tastier.

106. For an artist, withdrawal is necessary. (p. 96)

107. An artist requires the upkeep of creative solitude, the healing of time alone. Without this period of recharging, we become depleted. (p. 97)

108. There are powerful payoffs to be found in staying stuck and deferring nurturing your sense of self. (p. 97)

109. Many of us have made a virtue out of deprivation. We have embraced a long-suffering artistic anorexia as a martyr's cross. (p. 98)

110. Afraid to appear selfish, we lose our self. (p. 98)

111. Many people, caught in the virtue trap, do not appear to be self-destructive to the casual eye. (p. 99)

112. *The question is "Are you self-destructive?" not "Do you appear self-destructive?" (p. 99)*

113. We listen to other people's ideas of what is self-destructive without ever looking at whether their self and our self have similar needs. (p. 100)

114. One of the favored tricks of blocked creatives is saying no to ourselves.
(p. 101)

115. For many of us, raised to believe that money is the real source of security, a dependence on God feels foolhardy, suicidal, even laughable. When we consider the lilies of the fields, we think they are quaint, too out of it for the modern world.

(p. 105)

116. Listening to the siren song of more, we are deaf to the still small voice waiting in our soul to whisper, "You're enough."
(p. 105)

117. Many of us equate difficulty with virtue—and art with fooling around.
(p. 106)

118. We have tried to be sensible—as though we have any proof at all that God is sensible. (p. 107)

119. As you expect God to be more generous, God will be able to be more generous to you. (p. 108)

120. Because art is born in expansion, in a belief in sufficient supply, it is critical that we pamper ourselves for the sense of abundance it brings to us. (p. 108)

121. There is no monetary equivalent to joy. (Mark Bryan)

122. In order to thrive as artists—and, one could argue, as people—we need to be available to the universal flow. When we put a stopper on our capacity for joy by anorectically declining the small gifts of life, we turn aside the larger gifts as well. (p. 110)

123. *What gives us true joy? That is the question to ask concerning luxury.* (p. 110)

124. For many blocked creatives, it takes a little work to even imagine *ourselves having luxury. (p. 111)*

125. *What we are talking about when we discuss luxury is very often a shift in consciousness more than flow. (p. 111)*

126. Creative living requires the luxury of time, which we carve out for ourselves—even if it's fifteen minutes for quick morning pages and a ten-minute minibath after work. (p. 112)

*T*his week, we begin focusing on a deep, quiet inner listening, what the prayerful might call contemplation. We are turning away from the hurly-burly of the external world, seeking to hear our own dreams, goals, and desires. This we have been doing ever since we undertook our pages. This week, however, we are listening with greater specificity.

For many of us, the admission of a dream brings us squarely up against our own inner perfectionist. We dream, briefly, of what we'd like to do, and then we conjure immediately the nightmare specter of how poorly it would probably work out! We no sooner think, "I'd love to direct a little local theater piece," "I'd love to take an oil painting class," than we muster up the hundred reasons why we can't. We compare our baby steps to the masterpieces of acknowledged greats and we stop in our tracks.

Believing our "can'ts," it's a short hop, skip, and jump to jealousy of those who can. Jealousy is a cunning block. We are ashamed to feel it, and so we hide it. Hidden, it comes out sideways as sniping. "He's not so great," we think, feeling less than great ourselves.

The task this week is to listen both to the murmur of our dreams and the whisper of our jealousies. Both point us toward True North. It can fairly be said that *we* are True North, aiming home to the heart by listening to its tattooed truths.

127. Creative living requires the luxury of space for ourselves, even if all we manage to carve out is one special book-shelf and a windowsill that is ours. (p. 112)

128. Buy a small pocket notepad and write down every nickel you spend. Are you spending in ways that nurture you? (p. 112)

129. For many of us, counting is a necessary prelude to learning creative luxury. (p. 112)

130. *Art is not about thinking something up. It is about the opposite—getting something down. (p. 117)*

131. If we are trying to think something up, *we are straining to reach for something that's just beyond our grasp.* (p. 117)

132. When we get something down, there is no strain. We're not doing; we're getting. (p. 117)

133. Once you accept that it is natural to create, you can begin to accept a second idea—that the creator will hand you whatever you need for the project. The minute you are willing to accept the help of this collaborator, you will see useful bits of help everywhere in your life. Be alert: there is a second voice, a higher harmonic, adding to and augmenting your inner creative voice. This voice frequently shows itself in synchronicity. (p. 119)

134. Perfectionism is a refusal to let yourself move ahead. (p. 119)

135. For the perfectionist, there are no first drafts, rough sketches, warm-up exercises. (p. 120)

136. The perfectionist is never satisfied. (p. 120)

137. We always do the best that we can by the light we have to see by.

(p. 120)

138. QUESTION: What would I do if I didn't have to do it perfectly? ANSWER: A great deal more than I am. (p. 121)

139. In order to risk, we must jettison our accepted limits. (p. 121)

140. Usually, when we say we can't do something, what we mean is that we won't do something unless we can guarantee that we'll do it perfectly. (p. 121)

141. Very often a risk is worth taking simply for the sake of taking it. There is something enlivening about expanding our self-definition. (p. 123)

142. *"If I didn't have to do it perfectly, I would try . . ."* (p. 123)

143. Jealousy is a map. (p. 123)

144. Jealousy is always a mask
for fear: fear that we aren't
able to get what we want;
frustration that somebody else
seems to be getting what is
rightfully ours . . . (p. 124)

145. *At its root, jealousy is a stingy emotion. (p. 124)*

146. There is room for all of us. (p. 124)

147. As a kid, I missed the chance to . . . (p. 125)

*A*n ongoing creative life closely resembles an athletic career. Strength is gained from consistency, not from dramatic sprints. (A rule among many marathoners is ten slow miles for every one fast mile.)

As recovering creatives, we must learn how to move gently through our creative shinsplints. On the days when you feel strained muscles, battered, and ready to quit, give yourself a light day instead. Show up at your creative projects, but with very low expectations. Think of it as the spiritual equivalent of aerobic exercise. Even twenty minutes will be enough to maintain your soul by putting it in the target zone.

By now, a great deal of recovery has happened, and ironically, the temptation to self-sabotage may be rearing its head.

Teaching the Artist's Way as a twelve-week class, week eight is where dropout and rebellion most typically rear their heads. Sometimes rebellion is disguised as "What's the use?" Sometimes it's another wave of anger. "All that wasted time," we think. "So much pain. So much loss! I'm just too old for all this!"

If we could, we'd like to wriggle off the hook of our own creativity. We'd like to be "normal," by which we mean dreamless. We'd like very much to resign from taking risks—which means we're getting ready to take them again, and we're squinting at the jumps.

A word of advice here: Lower the jumps. Make a list of small, doable changes and execute those. Buy a new houseplant. Polish your shoes. Get new shoelaces for your running shoes. Keep things simple and fill the form you are in. Your rebellion will pass if you let yourself ride it out with tiny triumphs.

148. Artistic losses can be turned into artistic gains and strengths—but not in the isolation of the beleaguered artist's brain. (p. 129)

149. *In order to move through loss and beyond it, we must acknowledge it and share it. Because artistic losses are seldom openly acknowledged or mourned, they become artistic scar tissue that blocks artistic growth.*
(p. 129)

150. We must remember that our artist is a child and that what we can handle intellectually far outstrips what we can handle emotionally.
(p. 130)

151. The unmourned disappointment becomes the barrier that separates us from future dreams. (p. 130)

152. Many academics are themselves artistic beings who are deeply frustrated by their inability to create. Skilled in intellectual discourse, distanced by that intellectual skill from their own creative urgings, they often find the creativity of their charges deeply disturbing. (p. 131)

153. Creativity cannot be comfortably quantified in intellectual terms. (p. 132)

154. *For an artist, to become overly cerebral is to become crippled. (p. 132)*

155. Artists and intellectuals are not the same animal. (p. 132)

156. The lack of audacity—pinched out by critical abuse or malnourished through neglect—may cripple many artists far superior to those we publicly acclaim. (p. 133)

157. *Like the career of any athlete, an artist's life will have its injuries. (p. 134)*

158. Give yourself the dignity of admitting your artistic wounds.
(p. 134)

159. After the "Ouch!" say, "How can this loss serve me? Where does it point my work?" (p. 135)

160. *The trick is to metabolize pain as energy. (p. 135)*

161. Whenever I am willing to ask, "What is necessary next?" I have moved ahead. (p. 136)

162. *The key to career resiliency is self-empowerment and choice. The trick is to say, "What else could I do?" instead of "Why me?" (p. 136)*

163. When faced with a loss, immediately take one small action to support your artist. (p. 137)

164. QUESTION: Do you know how old I'll be by the time I learn to play the piano? ANSWER: The same age you will be if you don't. (p. 138)

165. *"I'm too old" is something we tell ourselves to save ourselves from the emotional cost of the ego deflation involved in being a beginner.* (p. 138)

166. Creativity occurs in the moment, and in the moment we are timeless.
(p. 139)

167. Instead of allowing ourselves a creative journey, we focus on the length of the trip. (p. 139)

168. At the heart of the anorexia of artistic avoidance is the denial of process.
(p. 139)

*I*f you have succeeded in putting most of your rebellion behind you, you may now be face-to-face with what it was masking: your fear. Admit your fear, embrace it, and be gentle with yourself. Rather than contempt for our fearful selves, we are aiming for a sense of compassion.

Fear is what causes all manner of self-destructive behaviors. First and foremost, fear causes us to balk. When we balk, we call ourselves "lazy," and a tirade of self-abuse begins. Do not call yourself lazy if you find yourself stalling. Accept that you are fearful and work with your fear instead.

It may be clear to you now how many times you have allowed fear to persuade you into taking creative U-turns. Try to be gentle with yourself. As time goes on, you can begin to undo some of them. For right now, you must begin with the compassion to forgive yourself for them all.

"But I'll never forgive myself," you may be thinking. "They asked me to make a few simple manuscript changes and resubmit the novel, and that was twenty years ago!" Old novels can be resuscitated. New novels can be begun, but only in an atmosphere of compassion.

Remember that the creative part of you is an inner youngster. Youngsters are easily embarrassed. They have a terrible fear of exposure. Only by acknowledging the fears of our artist-child can we begin to soothe and disarm them.

One of the most toxic ideas our culture perpetuates is that somewhere there is a tribe of elite—the "real" artists—and that this elite is *beyond fear*. No one is beyond fear. As artists, we must learn to move through our fears. As actress Julianna McCarthy points out accurately, "If you lose your vulnerability, you lose your capacity to be an artist."

There is a trick to living with our vulnerability, and that trick is compassion.

169. Creativity lies not in the done but in doing. (p. 139)

170. Focused on process, our creative life retains a sense of adventure. Focused on product, the same creative life can feel foolish or barren. We inherit the obsession with product and the idea that art produces finished product from our consumer-oriented society. (p. 139)

171. Ask yourself if you can acquire the humility to start something despite your ego's reservations. (p. 140)

172. Most of the time, the next right thing is something small: washing out your paintbrushes, stopping by the art supply store and getting your clay, checking the local paper for a list of acting classes. (p. 141)

173. All too often, when people look to having a more creative life, they hold an unspoken and often unacknowledged expectation, or fear, that they will be abandoning life as they know it.
(p. 141)

174. Blocked creatives like to think they are looking at changing their whole life in one fell swoop. This form of grandiosity is very often its own undoing. (p. 141)

175. Creativity requires activity, and this is not good news to most of us.
(p. 142)

176. In a creative career, thinking about the odds is a drink of emotional poison. (p. 142)

177. The odds are what we use to procrastinate about doing what comes next. (p. 142)

178. Most blocked creatives have an active addiction to anxiety. (p. 143)

179. Filling the form means that we must work with what we have rather than languish in complaints over what we have not. (p. 143)

180. Take one small daily action instead of indulging in the big questions.
(p. 143)

181. Make changes, small changes, right where you are. (p. 144)

182. Children may be told they can't do anything or, equally damaging, be told they should be able to do absolutely anything with ease. Either of these messages blocks the recipient. (p. 144)

183. One of the most important tasks in artistic recovery is learning to call things—and ourselves—by the right names. (p. 151)

184. *Blocked artists are not lazy. They are blocked. (p. 151)*

185. Do not call the inability to start laziness. Call it fear. (p. 152)

186. *The need to be a great artist makes it hard to be an artist. (p. 152)*

187. *The need to produce a great work of art makes it hard to produce any art at all. (p. 152)*

188. Being an artist requires enthusiasm more than discipline. Enthusiasm is not an emotional state. It is a spiritual commitment, a loving surrender to our creative process. (p. 153)

189. Enthusiasm (from the Greek, "filled with God") is an ongoing energy supply tapped into the flow of life itself. (p. 153)

*T*rue success is a gentle commodity built by evading internal blocks *and* external enemies. In other words, it is established through developing a healthy sense of self-protection. This means we need to be not only compassionate but also honest and vigilant with ourselves.

Many of the deadliest foes to creative outflow are internal, not external, challenges. Many of us are frightened by the velocity of creative energy, and so when we feel it, we pick up a familiar block to slow the flow. Our block may be food, drugs, sex, alcohol, work, or a potent cocktail combining several of the above. By now, you probably know which blocks, if any, are a problem for you. A sense of self-protection requires that you acknowledge them.

Gerry, a gifted poet, uses much of his creativity pursuing a hectic love life. Anna, a gifted writer, adds pounds instead of pounding the keys. Maggie, a healer with a gift for music, drowns all of it out with the jackhammer of overwork.

Any of these blocks can create a sense of "Oh, what's the use?" Like two other potent drugs, fame and competition, they tell us, "If *it* hasn't happened yet, *it* will never happen."

The *it,* of course, is success. Not the success of a quiet day's work well done, but the roaring tabloid success of the American Dream turned to headlines. This form of success is really an addiction to revenge: "I'll show them." What we mean by that is, "I'll show them *up.*"

If, in self-survey, you can now acknowledge using internal blocks to shut down or avoid your creative flow, this may be the week where you gently set such blocks aside.

190. As attractive as the idea of a pristine cell, monastic in its severity, is to our romanticized notion of being a real artist, the workable truth may be somewhat messier than that. Most little kids would be bored silly in a stark, barren room. Our artist child is no exception.
(p. 154)

191. Recovering from artist's block, like recovering from any major illness or injury, requires a commitment to health. (p. 154)

192. We usually commit creative hara-kiri either on the eve of or in the wake of a first creative victory. (p. 154)

193. *An artistic U-turn arrives on a sudden wave of indifference. (p. 155)*

194. In dealing with our creative U-turns, we must first of all extend ourselves some sympathy. Creativity is scary, and in all careers there are U-turns. (p. 156)

195. Typically, when we take a creative U-turn, we are doubly shamed: first by our fear and second by our reaction to it.

(p. 156)

196. Have compassion. Creative U-turns are always born from fear. (p. 157)

197. To recover from a creative U-turn, or a pattern involving many creative U-turns, we must first admit that it exists. Yes, I did react negatively to fear and pain. Yes, I do need help. (p. 157)

198. Once we admit the need for help, the help arrives. (p. 157)

199. In order to work freely on a project, an artist must be at least functionally free of resentment (anger) and resistance (fear). (p. 158)

200. Remember, your artist is a creative child. It sulks, throws tantrums, holds grudges, harbors irrational fears. (p. 158)

201. Creativity is God energy flowing through us, shaped by us, like light flowing through a crystal prism. (p. 163)

202. Every creative person has myriad ways to block creativity. Each of us favors one or two ways, particularly toxic to us because they block us so effectively. (p. 163)

203. Food, work, and sex are all good in themselves. It is the abuse of them that makes them creativity issues. Knowing yourself as an artist means acknowledging which of these you abuse when you want to block yourself. (p. 164)

204. Blocking is essentially an issue of faith. Rather than trust our intuition, our talent, our skill, our desire, we fear where our creator is taking us with this creativity. (p. 165)

205. *Workaholism is an addiction, and like all addictions, it blocks creative energy. (p. 166)*

206. The phrase "I'm working" has a certain unassailable air of goodness and duty to it. The truth is, we are very often working to avoid ourselves, our spouses, our real feelings. (p. 166)

207. In order to recover our creativity, we must learn to see workaholism as a block instead of a building block.
(p. 168)

208. *There is a treadmill quality to workaholism.* (p. 168)

209. Droughts tell us that they will last forever—and that we will not. During a drought, the morning pages seem both painful and foolish. (p. 170)

210. In a creative life, droughts are a necessity. The time in the desert brings us clarity and charity. When you are in a drought, know that it is to a purpose. And keep writing morning pages. (p. 171)

As long as we allow our self-worth to be dependent on someone else's evaluation—the fat paycheck, the one-man show, the *New Yorker* short-story sale—we are depriving ourselves of our own dignity and our own autonomy. Art is a process, not a product.

"But, Julia, I'm not making any money at my art," you may protest. "Real artists make a living off their art!"

Hooey. Tell that to Gauguin, Van Gogh, Walt Whitman, Emily Dickinson. . . . Stop looking at the marketplace and start looking at the gains you have made in practicing your art. Please be gentle with yourself. A sense of self-tenderness allows the artist-child increased freedom to explore. Art flourishes in an atmosphere of self-acceptance. It is up to each of us to establish this atmosphere for ourselves. That is true autonomy.

We need to divorce our value as artists from the cash flow our art generates. In our society, this is not an easy thing to do. Even when we read about other artists, the news "hook" tends to be monetary: the $800,000 novel advance, the $3.5 million screenplay, the $12 million salary for acting in a film.

Although many of us do make money at it, creativity is its own reward. Too often, contemplating a new piece of work, we think, "Where will this get me?"

We want a cash-on-the-barrelhead, linear response, but creativity doesn't work that way. Very often it is the stray tendril, the curious wisp of a trail that leads us into new creative growth. Creativity moves in spurts, bursts, spirals. Today's "dead end" may be necessary to tomorrow's breakthrough.

To lead autonomous lives, we must engage in following our creative impulses freely, not second-guessing them, not ruling out the oddball urge that doesn't seem to "go anywhere."

"Anywhere" must come to be defined as "Anywhere *I'd* like to go."

Remember: Art equals *all real things*.

211. *Our culture's addiction to fame encourages us to believe that if it hasn't happened yet, it won't happen. (p. 171)*

212. *Fame is a spiritual drug. (p. 171)*

213. The point of the work is the work. (p. 171)

214. Competition is another spiritual drug. When we focus on competition we poison our own well, impede our own progress. (p. 172)

215. Competition lies at the root of much creative blockage. Comparing ourselves to others, we think, "What's the use?" (p. 173)

216. As artists, we cannot afford to think about who is getting ahead of us and how they don't deserve it. The desire to be better than can choke off the simple desire to be.
(p. 173)

217. *The footrace mentality is always the ego's demand to be not just good but also first and best. (p. 174)*

218. It is the accurate mapping out of our own creative interests that invites the term "original." We are the "origin" of our art, its homeland. Viewed this way, originality is the process of remaining true to ourselves. (p. 174)

219. Art needs time to incubate, to sprawl a little, to be ungainly and misshapen, and finally emerge as itself. The ego hates this fact. (p. 175)

220. *As an artist, I may need a different mix of stability and flow than other people. (p. 179)*

*221. I have to free myself
from determining my value
and the value of my work
by my work's market value.
(p. 179)*

222. I need to create what wants to be created. (p. 180)

223. As an artist, I must be very careful to surround myself with people who nurture my artist—not people who try to overly domesticate it for my own good.
(p. 180)

224. As an artist, my self-respect comes from doing the work. (p. 180)

225. I show up at the morning pages and I write about my ugly curtains, my rotten haircut, my delight in the way the light hit the trees on the morning run. All parts of me are welcome there.
(p. 181)

226. *There is a connection between self-nurturing and self-respect.* (p. 181)

227. Creativity is a spiritual practice. It is not something that can be perfected, finished, and set aside. (p. 182)

228. We are asked to expand in order that we not contract. (p. 182)

229. As artists, we are spiritual sharks. The ruthless truth is that if we don't keep moving, we sink to the bottom and die. (p. 182)

230. The stringent requirement of a sustained creative life is the humility to start again, to begin anew. (p. 182)

231. As artists, we are travelers. (p. 183)

*C*reativity is a matter of faith, and "faith without works is dead." We reach an end only to find it is a beginning. We draw a conclusion only to find it poses a question. We are never finished.

In nearing the end of this journal, you have only begun to tap the potential within you. As my longtime partner Mark Bryan often remarks, "Beginning morning pages is like altering the trajectory of a space launch by two degrees. It looks like a negligible difference until you carry it out for a couple of years. Then you see it's the difference between Mars and Jupiter."

Many of our students have been working with morning pages for years now. I recently received a letter from Michael, who began working with them when he was blocked as an actor and alienated from his life in the theater. It is now five years later, and Michael writes that he is back on track, acting and successfully directing. A famous theater in Chicago has sent him to London and Paris to scout shows, and yes, he uses his morning pages and his artist dates regularly.

The Artist's Way is a spiritual practice, and you are a spiritual practitioner. Our spiritual practice may evolve and change, but abandoning it amounts to abandoning yourself. Morning pages may not be your ultimate spiritual path, but continued work with them may lead you to where you're going.

It isn't unusual to mutiny briefly at the end of the first twelve weeks. Morning pages do get abandoned. Artist dates become memories. Life goes back to regular life, except . . . morning pages and artist dates had *become* regular life. Dreadful as it sounds, we miss them a little. More to the point, we miss *us*.

This is where faith comes in: the faith to experiment again with a renewed use of the tools. If you experiment and observe, you too may come to believe that morning pages and artist dates are an effective way to communicate with the universe, and that if we communicate, Something or Someone communicates back.

232. Creativity is not a business, although it may generate much business.

(p. 183)

233. You don't need to overturn a successful career in order to find creative fulfillment. It is *necessary* to overturn each day's schedule slightly to allow for those small adjustments in daily trajectory that, over the long haul, alter the course and the satisfactions of our careers. (p. 184)

234. Art requires some considered risk. Attempting to insure our finances by playing it safe, we lose our cutting edge. Being too stingy with our artist is anorexia. (p. 184)

235. Creativity requires action, and part of that action must be physical.
(p. 185)

236. Art requires attention. One quickly notes that when the mind is focused on other, *the self often comes into a far more accurate focus. (p. 185)*

237. Exercise is often what moves us from stagnation to inspiration, from problem to solution, from self-pity to self-respect. (p. 189)

238. Remember that your artist is fed by images. We need to unlearn our old notion that spirituality and sensuality don't mix.
(p. 189)

239. Small rituals, self-devised, are good for the soul. (p. 189)

240. Remember, the artist child speaks the language of the soul: music, dance, scent, shells... Your artist's altar to the creator should be fun to look at, even silly. Remember how much little kids like gaudy stuff. Your artist is a little kid, so a bit of gawdy frippery might be called for. (p. 190)

241. Creativity requires faith. Faith requires that we relinquish control. (p. 193)

242. *We are not accustomed to thinking that God's will for us and our own inner dreams can coincide. (p. 194)*

243. It is the inner commitment to be true to ourselves and follow our dreams that triggers the support of the universe. (p. 194)

244. *Creativity—like human life itself—begins in darkness.* (p. 194)

245. We speak often about ideas as brainchildren. What we do not realize is that brainchildren, like all babies, should not be dragged from the creative womb prematurely. (p. 194)

246. Mystery is at the heart of creativity. That, and surprise . . . As creative channels, we need to trust the darkness. (p. 195)

247. *Hatching an idea is a lot like baking bread. An idea needs time to rise. (p. 195)*

248. We are an ambitious society, and it is often difficult for us to cultivate forms of creativity that do not directly serve us and our career goals. Recovery urges reexamining our definitions of creativity and expanding them to include what in the past we called hobbies. (p. 196)

249. As gray, as controlled, as dreamless as we may strive to be, the fire of our dreams will not stay buried. The embers are always there, stirring in our frozen souls. (p. 197)

250. *Just when we are ready to achieve escape velocity, we draw to ourselves the Test.*

251. A little flattery can go a long way toward deterring our escape velocity. So can a little cash. More sinister than either is the impact a well-placed doubt can have, particularly a "for your own good, just wanted to make sure you've thought about this" doubt—voiced by one of our nearest and dearest. (p. 199)

252. Do not indulge or tolerate anyone who throws cold water in your direction. (p. 200)

When *The Artist's Way* was first published, I expressed a wish for Artist's Way groups to spring into being. I envisioned them as peer-run circles—"creative clusters"—where people would serve each other as believing mirrors, uniting with the common aim of creative unblocking. It was my vision that such circles would be free of charge, that anyone could assemble one, using the book as a guide and a text. Many such peer-run circles did form and many more are forming still. Such artist-to-artist, heart-to-heart help and support is the heart of *The Artist's Way* and *The Vein of Gold.*

Not surprisingly, many therapists, community colleges, wellness centers, universities, and teachers soon began running facilitated Artist's Way groups, for which they charged a fee. The Artist's Way groups were led rather than simply convened. To the degree to which they adhered to the spiritual principles of creative recovery and introduced people to the use of the tools, they were—and are—valuable. Any group that starts with such a leader should, however, rapidly become autonomous, "graduating" to a peer-run, non-profit status.

There are no "accredited" Artist's Way teachers. I chose not to franchise *The Artist's Way,* but to offer it as a gift, free of charge. It is my belief that creative recovery at its best is a nonhierarchical, peer-run, collective process. In this it differs from the academic and therapeutic models. Any professional using *The Artist's Way* should realize that autonomous, peer-run creative clusters must remain the eventual goal. Facilitated groups can serve as a sort of bridge to this end.

In my years of teaching and traveling, I have frequently encountered excellent results from peer-group clusters. On occasion, I have encountered situations where *The Artist's Way* has been unduly modified. Whenever there is a misplaced emphasis on intellectual "analysis" or therapeutic "processing," there is the risk of undermining creative unfolding. Very often, what could be interpreted as "neurosis" or a deep-seated problem is simply creative resistance.

Both *The Artist's Way* and *The Vein of Gold* are experiential books. They are intended to teach people to process and transform life through acts of creativity. Both books and *all* creative clusters should be practiced through creative action, not through theory. As an artist, I know this. *The Artist's Way* and *The Vein of Gold* are the distillate of thirty years of artistic practice.

It is my belief and my experience as a teacher that all of us are healthy enough to practice creativity. It is not a dangerous endeavor requiring trained facilitators. It is our human birthright and something we can do gently and collectively. Creativity is like breathing—pointers may help, but *we do the process ourselves*. Creative clusters, where we gather as peers to develop our strength, are best regarded as tribal gatherings, where creative beings raise, celebrate, and actualize the creative power which runs through us all.

Guidelines

1. Use a Twelve-Week Process with a Weekly Gathering of Two to Three Hours. The morning pages and artist dates are required of everyone in the group, including facilitators. The exercises are done in order in the group, with everyone, including the facilitator, answering the questions and then sharing the answers in clusters of four, one chapter per week. Do not share your morning pages with the group or anyone else. Do not reread your morning pages until later in the course, if you are required to do so by your facilitator or your own inner guidance.

2. Avoid Self-Appointed Gurus. If there is any emissary, it is the work itself, as a collective composed of all who take the course, at home or otherwise. Each person is equally a part of the collective, no one more than another. While there may be "teachers," facilitators, who are relied on during the twelve-week period to guide others down the path, such facilitators need to be prepared to share their own material and take their own creative risks. This is a dialectic rather than a monologue—an egalitarian group process rather than a hierarchical one.

3. Listen. We each get what we need from the group process by sharing our own material and by listening to others. We do not need to comment on another person's sharing in order to help that person. We must refrain from trying to "fix" someone else. Each group devises a cooperative creative "song" of artistic recovery. Each group's song is unique to that group—like that of a pod or family of whales, initiating and echoing to establish their position. When listening, go around the circle without commenting unduly on what is heard. The circle, as a shape, is very important. We are intended to witness, not control, one another. When sharing exercises, small clusters of four within the larger groups are important: five tends to become unwieldy in terms of time constraints; three doesn't allow for enough contrasting experience. Obviously, not all groups can be divided into equal fours. Just try and do so whenever you can.

4. Respect One Another. Be certain that respect and compassion are afforded equally to every member. Each person must be able to speak his own wounds and dreams. No one is to be "fixed" by another member of the group. This is a deep and powerful internal process. There is no one right way to do this. Love is important. Be kind to yourself. Be kind to one another.

5. Expect Change in the Group Makeup. Many people will— some will not—fulfill the twelve-week process. There is often a rebellious or fallow period after the twelve weeks, with people returning to the disciplines later. When they do, they continue to find the process unfolding within them a year, a few years, or many years later. Many groups have a tendency to drive apart at eight to ten weeks (creative U-turns) because of the feelings of loss associated with the group's ending. Face that truth as a group; it may help you stay together.

6. Be Autonomous. You cannot control your own process, let alone anyone else's. Know that you will feel rebellious occasionally—that you won't want to do all of your morning pages and exercises at different times in the twelve weeks. Relapse is okay. You cannot do this process perfectly, so relax, be kind to yourself, and hold on to your hat. Even when you feel nothing is happening, you will be changing at great velocity. This change is a deepening into your own intuition, your own creative self. The structure of the course is about safely getting across the bridge into new realms of creative spiritual awareness.

7. Be Self-Loving. If the facilitator feels somehow "wrong" to you, change clusters or start your own. Continually seek your own inner guidance rather than outer guidance. You are seeking to form an artist-to-artist relationship with the Great Creator. Keep gurus at bay. You have your own answers within you.

A Word To Therapists, Teachers, Writing Instructors, and Other Artist's Way Group Leaders. Thank you for the wonderful work you do. While I know that many of you are using *The Artist's Way* to run groups,

I hope and expect that you will go on to explore your own interests using *The Artist's Way* for your process, also. I encourage you to follow your own creative vision, to strive for your own True North. You will find that the facilitation process continues your own growth experience.

I cannot state emphatically enough that *The Artist's Way* fame and path should not be used in ways that differ substantially from the Artist's Way techniques as spelled out in the book. I have tested the tools for a decade and a half in order to find them roadworthy. I ask that you refrain from presenting yourselves publicly as Artist's Way "experts," though you may use the book within your practice. I ask that you remember that the wisdom of *The Artist's Way* is a collective, nonhierarchical experience. I have heard of abuses of this principle, such as a group leader's requiring the morning pages to be read in the group. This is not in the spirit of the book. Facilitated groups should "graduate" into free, peer-run clusters.

A Word to Therapeutic Clients. Please remember that the book itself remains the primary source of the Artist's Way teachings, and that it is your interpretation, and your work with the book and its tools, that are central to you in your recovery. I remind you that the work is your own, not just something done under the influence of a magic teacher. Please "own" your recovery as your recovery.

Thank You. I am delighted *The Artist's Way* is used in the many contexts in which it is (such as colleges and universities, by therapists, by peer-run clusters). I again offer the reminder that the Artist's Way is intended to be used in keeping with the spirit of the book, as written. There is always the book itself to refer to. This is an individual's journey that may be facilitated by the group process. If you cannot find or start a group, consider you and the book to comprise one!

Pass It On. To those forming a peer-run cluster, you do not need to make the Artist's Way a money-making venture, for me or for you. If you follow the spiritual practice of tithing, we recommend buying the book and passing it on.

Introduction

Although creative recovery is a highly individual process, there are certain recurrent themes and questions that we have encountered over and over in our teaching. In the hopes of answering at least some of your questions directly, we include the most commonly asked questions and answers here.

Questions and Answers

Q: *Is true creativity the possession of a relatively small percentage of the population?*

A: No, absolutely not. We all are creative. Creativity is a natural life force that all can experience, in one form or another. Just as blood is part of our physical body and is nothing we must invent, creativity is part of us and we each can tap into the greater creative energies of the universe and pull from that vast, powerful spiritual wellspring to amplify our own individual creativity.

As a culture, we tend to define creativity too narrowly and to think of it in elitist terms, as something belonging to a small chosen tribe of "real artists." But in reality, everything we do requires making creative choices, although we seldom recognize that fact. The ways in which we dress, set up our homes, do our jobs, the movies we see, and even the people we involve ourselves with—these all are expressions of our creativity. It is our erroneous beliefs about creativity, our cultural mythology about artists ("All artists are broke, crazy, promiscuous, self-centered, single, or they have trust funds") that encourage us to leave our dreams unfulfilled. These myths most often involve matters of money, time, and other people's agendas for us. As we clear these blocks away, we can become more creative.

Q: *What factors keep people from being creative?*

A: Conditioning. Family, friends, and educators may discourage us from pursuing an artist's career. There is the mythology that artists are somehow "different," and this mythology of difference inspires fear. If we have negative perceptions about what an artist is, we will feel less inclined to do the diligent work necessary to become one.

On a societal level, blocked creative energy manifests itself as self-destructive behavior. Many people who are engaged in self-defeating behaviors, such as addicts of alcohol, drugs, sex, or work, are really in the hands of this shadow side of the creative force. As we become more creative, these negative expressions of the creative force often abate.

Q: *How does this book free people to be more creative?*

A: The primary purpose—and effect—of *The Artist's Way* is to put people in touch with the power of their own internal creativity. The book frees people to be more creative in many different ways: First, it helps dismantle negative mythologies about artists. Second, it helps people discover their own creative force, access it, and express it more freely. Third, it provides people with an awareness about their self-destructive behaviors and allows them to see more clearly what the impediments on their individual path might be. Finally, the book helps people identify and celebrate their desires and dreams and make the plans to accomplish them. It teaches people how to support and nurture themselves as well as how to find others who will support them in fulfilling their dreams.

Q: *One of the central themes of* The Artist's Way *is the link between creativity and spirituality. How are they connected?*

A: Creativity is a spiritual force. The force that drives the green fuse through the flower, as Dylan Thomas defined his idea of the life force, is the same urge that drives us toward creation. There is a central will to create that is part of our human heritage and potential. Because creation is always an act of faith, and faith is a spiritual issue, so is creativity. As we strive for our highest selves, our spiritual selves, we cannot help but be more aware, more proactive, and more creative.

Q: *Tell me about the two central exercises in the book—the morning pages and the artist dates.*

A: The morning pages are three pages of stream-of-consciousness longhand morning writing. You should think of them not as "art" but as an active form of meditation for Westerners. In the morning pages we declare to the world—and ourselves—what we like, what we dislike, what we wish, what we hope, what we regret, and what we plan.

By contrast, the artist dates are times for receptivity, preplanned solitary hours of pleasurable activity aimed at nurturing the creative consciousness. Used together, these tools build, in effect, a radio set.

The morning pages notify and clarify—they send signals into the verdant void; and the solitude of the artist dates allows for the answer to be received.

The morning pages and artist dates must be experienced in order to be explained, just as reading a book about jogging is not the same as putting on your Nikes and heading out to the running track. Map is not territory, and without reference points from within your own experience, you cannot extrapolate what the morning pages and artist dates can do for you.

Q: The Artist's Way *is a twelve-week program that requires daily commitments. How much time do I need to devote to it each day, and what can I accomplish in these twelve weeks?*

A: It's a daily commitment of a half hour to an hour. One of the most important things we learn during the twelve weeks is to give up our ideas of perfection and to see a new perspective, to change our focus from product to process.

Participants enter the program with certain unstated expectations and preconceived notions of what will happen and what they will get out of it. And often, just as in a great short story, they are profoundly surprised and thrilled to discover something entirely different. Therefore, to predict what someone will learn from this course would undermine the very principle on which it was built. It is experiential, and the results are something to be discovered, not explained.

Q: *What can I do to overcome my self-doubts about being a good artist?*

A: The point is not to *overcome* your self-doubts about being an artist. The point is to *move through* your self-doubts. Many of us believe that "real artists" do not experience self-doubt. In truth, artists are people who have learned to live with doubt and do the work anyway. The exercises in the book will help you dismantle the hypercritical inner Censor and perfectionist. You will learn that part of being fully creative means allowing for an "off" day. Because the Artist's Way focuses on process rather than product, you will learn to value your "mistakes" as part of your learning.

Q: *Why do artists procrastinate, and what is procrastination really about?*

A: Artists procrastinate out of fear, or because they try to wait for the "right mood" in order to work. *The Artist's Way* will teach you how to separate mood from productivity. It will also teach you to value a self-loving enthusiasm over mechanistic discipline.

Q: *How can I expand my ability to derive new ideas?*

A: Learn to miniaturize your critic, your Censor. While you may not fire your critic entirely, you can learn to work around the negative voice. When we use the morning pages and the artist dates—specifically designed to put us in touch with our nonlinear intuitive selves—we expand our ability to derive new ideas. As we lessen the static, the interference caused by old habits and blocks, and become clearer and more able to listen, we become more receptive to creativity and its sometimes subtle arrival in our consciousness.

Q: *What is the most common misconception about creativity?*

A: The most common misconception is that we would have to leave our current lives in order to pursue our dreams. It is easier for us to use our jobs, families, financial situations, time obligations, etc., as a way (or ways) to keep us "safe" from the anxiety caused by stepping out of our comfort zones into the creative process. When we allow ourselves to be thus thwarted, we deny ourselves tremendous joy.

About the Author

Julia Cameron is the author of fifteen books, fiction and nonfiction, and many plays and movies. She happily lives in the high desert of New Mexico where she busies herself with musicals, movies, poetry, horses, and dogs. She has taught extensively for two decades in venues ranging from London to Los Angeles, from Esalen to *The New York Times.* Her work on creativity features the best selling books *The Artist's Way, The Vein of Gold, The Right to Write,* and *God Is No Laughing Matter.*

Discover more of yourself with Inner Work Books.

The following Inner Work Books are part of a series that explores psyche and spirit through writing, visualization, ritual, and imagination.

The Artist's Way: A Spiritual Path to Higher Creativity   BY JULIA CAMERON

At a Journal Workshop (revised edition): *Writing to Access the Power of the Unconscious and Evoke Creative Ability* BY IRA PROGOFF, PH.D.

Ending the Struggle Against Yourself: A Workbook for Developing Deep Confidence and Self-Acceptance BY STAN TAUBMAN, D.S.W.

Fearless Creating: A Step-by-Step Guide to Starting and Completing Your Work of Art   BY ERIC MAISEL, PH.D.

Finding What You Didn't Lose: Expressing Your Truth and Creativity Through Poem-Making   BY JOHN FOX

Following Your Path: Using Myths, Symbols, and Images to Explore Your Inner Life   BY ALEXANDRA COLLINS DICKERMAN

The Inner Child Workbook: What to Do with Your Past When It Just Won't Go Away   BY CATHRYN L. TAYLOR, M.A.M.F.C.C.

A Journey Through Your Childhood: A Write-in Guide for Reliving Your Past, Clarifying Your Present, and Charting Your Future   BY CHRISTOPHER BIFFLE

A Life in the Arts: Practical Guidance and Inspiration for Creative and Performing Artists   BY ERIC MAISEL, PH.D.

The Life We Are Given: A Long-Term Program for Realizing the Potential of Body, Mind, Heart, and Soul BY GEORGE LEONARD AND MICHAEL MURPHY

The Mythic Path: Discovering the Guiding Stories of Your Past—Creating a Vision for Your Future   BY DAVID FEINSTEIN, PH.D., AND STANLEY KRIPPNER, PH.D.

Pain and Possibility: Writing Your Way Through Personal Crisis   BY GABRIELE LUSSER RICO

The Path of the Everyday Hero: Drawing on the Power of Myth to Meet Life's Most Important Challenges BY LORNA CATFORD, PH.D., and MICHAEL RAY, PH.D.

The Possible Human: A Course in Extending Your Physical, Mental, and Creative Abilities   BY JEAN HOUSTON

The Search for the Beloved: Journeys in Mythology and Sacred Psychology   BY JEAN HOUSTON

Smart Love: A Codependence Recovery Program Based on Relationship Addiction Support Groups   BY JODY HAYES

Spiritual Passages: Embracing Life's Sacred Journey   BY DREW LEDER, M.D., PH.D.

A Time to Heal Workbook: Stepping-stones to Recovery for Adult Children of Alcoholics   BY TIMMEN L. CERMAK, M.D., AND JACQUES RUTZKY, M.F.C.C.

True Partners: A Workbook for Building a Lasting Intimate Relationship   BY TINA B. TESSINA, PH.D., AND RILEY K. SMITH, M.A.

The Vein of Gold: A Journey to Your Creative Heart   BY JULIA CAMERON

Writing from Life: Telling Your Soul's Story   BY SUSAN WITTIG ALBERT, PH.D.

Your Mythic Journey: Finding Meaning in Your Life Through Writing and Storytelling   BY SAM KEEN AND ANNE VALLEY-FOX

To order call 1-800-788-6262 or send your order to:

Jeremy P. Tarcher
Mail Order Department
The Putnam Berkley Group, Inc.
P.O. Box 12289
Newark, NJ 07101-5289

For Canadian orders:
P.O. Box 25000
Postal Station "A"
Toronto, Ontario M5W 2X8

____	The Artist's Way	0-87477-694-5	$14.95
____	The Artist's Way Hardcover Deluxe Edition	0-87477-821-2	$24.95
____	At a Journal Workshop	0-87477-638-4	$15.95
____	Ending the Struggle Against Yourself	0-87477-763-1	$14.95
____	Fearless Creating	0-87477-805-0	$15.95
____	Finding What You Didn't Lose	0-87477-909-3	$14.95
____	Following Your Path	0-87477-687-2	$15.95
____	The Inner Child Workbook	0-87477-635-X	$14.95
____	A Journey Through Your Childhood	0-87477-499-3	$10.95
____	A Life in the Arts	0-87477-766-6	$15.95
____	The Life We Are Given	0-87477-792-5	$14.95
____	The Mythic Path	0-87477-857-3	$17.95
____	Pain and Possibility	0-87477-571-X	$14.95
____	The Path of the Everyday Hero	0-87477-630-9	$14.95
____	The Possible Human	0-87477-872-7	$15.95
____	The Search for the Beloved	0-87477-871-9	$15.95
____	Smart Love	0-87477-472-1	$10.95
____	Spiritual Passages	0-87477-873-5	$15.95
____	A Time to Heal Workbook	0-87477-745-3	$14.95
____	True Partners	0-87477-727-5	$13.95
____	The Vein of Gold	0-87477-836-0	$20.95
____	Writing from Life	0-87477-848-4	$16.95
____	Your Mythic Journey	0-87477-543-4	$9.95

Subtotal $_____

Shipping and handling* $_____

Sales tax (CA, NJ, NY, PA, VA) $_____

Total amount due $_____

Payable in U.S. funds (no cash orders accepted). $15.00 minimum for credit card orders.

*Shipping and handling: $2.50 for one book, $0.75 for each additional book, not to exceed $6.25.

Enclosed is my   ❑ check   ❑ money order

Please charge my   ❑ Visa   ❑ MasterCard   ❑ American Express

Card # _____ Expiration date _____

Signature as on credit card _____

Daytime phone number _____

Name _____

Address _____

City _____ State_____ Zip_____

Please allow six weeks for delivery. Prices subject to change without notice.

Source key IWB